MATERIALS THAT MATTER

PAPER

Neil Morris

amicus

Published by Amicus
P.O. Box 1329
Mankato, MN 56002

Printed in the United States of America,
at Corporate Graphics in North Mankato, Minnesota

Library of Congress Cataloging-in-Publication Data
Morris, Neil, 1946-
  Paper / by Neil Morris.
    p. cm. -- (Materials that matter)
  Includes bibliographical references and index.
  Summary: "Discusses paper as a material, including historical uses,
current uses, manufacturing, and recycling"--Provided by publisher.
  ISBN 978-1-60753-067-1 (library binding)
  1. Paper--Juvenile literature. I. Title.
  TS1105.5.M65 2011
  676--dc22

                                                    2009051436

Created by Appleseed Editions Ltd.
Designed by Helen James
Edited by Mary-Jane Wilkins
Artwork by Graham Rosewarne
Picture research by Su Alexander

Photograph acknowledgements
Page 4 Neil Holmes Freelance Digital/Alamy; 5 Bill Barksdale/AgStock Images/Corbis;
6 INTERPHOTO/Alamy; 7 British Library/AKG; 8 Bettmann/Corbis; 9 Christopher Taylor/
Alamy; 10 Bill Brooks/Alamy; 11 Paul Almasy/Corbis; 12 Richard Bickel/Corbis; 13 David R Frazier
Photolibrary, Inc./Alamy; 14 Edward Parker/Alamy; 16 Robert Essel NYC/Corbis; 17 Eric Fowke/
Alamy; 18 ImageState/Alamy; 19 Coffeehouse Productions/Alamy; 20 British Library/The Art Archive;
21 epa/Corbis; 22 Walter Hodges/Corbis; 24 Gabe Palmer/Corbis; 25 Jose Luis Pelaez, Inc./Corbis;
26 Anna Clopet/Corbis; 27 Lester Lefkowitz/Corbis; 28 Enigma/Alamy; 29 Paolo Negri/Alamy
Front cover Robert Essel NYC/Corbis

DAD0041
32010

9 8 7 6 5 4 3 2 1

Contents

What Is Paper?

We all know what paper looks like. The pages of this book are made of paper, and so is the book's cover. If we give someone a book as a present, we might put it in colorful wrapping paper. Many other things are made of paper, including newspapers, magazines, writing pads, birthday cards, and toilet paper.

This supermarket sells a wide range of magazines on all sorts of subjects. Magazines, books, and newspapers are all made of paper.

All paper is made of millions of tiny **fibers**. These fibers are made of a plant substance called **cellulose**. We make paper by mixing cellulose fibers with water and turning them into a sheet that dries to form paper.

Small Cells

The word *cellulose* comes from the French *cellule*, meaning small cell. Scientists call cellulose a **carbohydrate**, which means that it is made up of **carbon**, **hydrogen**, and **oxygen**. Sugar and **starch** are also carbohydrates.

Cellulose forms the main part of the cell walls of plants, including trees and grasses. It makes up about one-third of all vegetable matter, but the exact amount varies. For example, cellulose makes up one-half of wood and nine-tenths of cotton. Cellulose fibers are tiny: about 0.004 inch (0.1 mm) wide and 0.05 inch (1.3 mm) long.

USE IT AGAIN AND AGAIN

All kinds of paper can be used again and again (see pages 24–27 on recycling). It is impossible to tell whether a book or newspaper is made from new or recycled paper. When we recycle paper, we help the environment. Every time we recycle a ton of paper:

- We use 3,000 to 4,000 kWh (**kilowatt hours**) less electricity than when making new paper (enough to power an average house for a year)
- We use 8,000 fewer gallons (30,000 L) of water
- We create 95 percent less air **pollution**

Hard and Soft Wood

The cellulose fibers used to make paper come mostly from trees. About three-quarters of papermaking wood comes from **softwood** trees. Many are specially grown for this. Paper manufacturers also use waste

TREES FOR MAKING PAPER

softwood	hardwood
fir	acacia
pine	aspen
spruce	birch
Western hemlock	eucalyptus
	maple
	oak
	poplar

and trimmings from trees that are cut down for other uses. Any unwanted wood is turned into wood chips, then pulped (see pages 12–13). Softwood comes from **coniferous** (cone-bearing, needle-leaved) trees. Their fibers are .08 to .16 inch (2–4mm) long and make strong paper. **Hardwood** comes from broad-leaved trees. Their shorter fibers are .02 to .06 inch (0.5–1.5 mm) long and make smoother paper.

Loggers cut down trees for building material as well as to make paper. These logs are being loaded onto a truck in a forest in Mississippi.

The First Paper

The word "paper" comes from papyrus, a reed that the ancient Egyptians used to make writing material. They cut papyrus stems into narrow strips and pressed them together into sheets, which they could then roll up. The sheets and rolls are also called papyri, and the oldest surviving examples are more than 5,000 years old.

Other ancient peoples used wood or bark for carving inscriptions. The word book comes from the Old English term *boc*, meaning beech tree. The first real paper was invented 2,000 years ago in ancient China.

The story of Cai Lun

A traditional Chinese story tells how a court official named Cai Lun (ca. AD 50–121) invented paper. Some historians believe that the first paper was actually made a few hundred years earlier and that Cai Lun just improved the way it was done. He belonged to the court of Emperor He (AD 79–105) of the Eastern Han dynasty and was unhappy with the writing materials that were available. Bamboo was heavy, and silk (another Chinese invention)

This eighteenth-century illustration shows the ancient Chinese method of making paper in wooden frames. Chinese craftsmen perfected their technique over centuries.

CHINESE PAPER

Cai Lun used the sides of a wooden box as a frame or **mold**. He fitted a screen into the box. This was probably made of woven cloth and was replaced by later papermakers with strips of bamboo. Cai Lun added water to make a slushy **pulp** from the bark and other ingredients. He poured the pulp onto the screen, stirred the solution, and then lifted the screen out of the frame, with a thin layer of wet pulp attached. He dried this in the sun for several hours, and it turned into a sheet of paper.

was precious and expensive. In AD 105 Cai Lun made paper by soaking various materials together in water. These included mulberry tree bark, stems of the **hemp** plant, old pieces of cloth (or silk) and fishing net rope. He then drained the water and let the material dry into a thin sheet of paper.

From Asia to Europe

The ancient Chinese realized how important their invention was, and they tried to keep it secret. This proved impossible though, and the technique had reached ancient Korea by the seventh century. It was then taken to Japan by **Buddhist** priests. In AD 751, the Chinese lost the Battle of Talas (in modern Kyrgyzstan) to the Arabs, and Chinese prisoners of war were forced to share their knowledge of papermaking.

By AD 793 there was a paper mill in the city of Baghdad (in modern Iraq). Papermaking had spread to Damascus (in modern Syria) by the time of the first **crusade** in 1096. European Christian knights then took the knowledge back to Europe, and the Moors also introduced the technology when they conquered Spain. By the fourteenth century mills were producing paper in Spain, France, Germany, and Italy.

This nineteenth-century illustration shows workers in an early Persian paper mill.

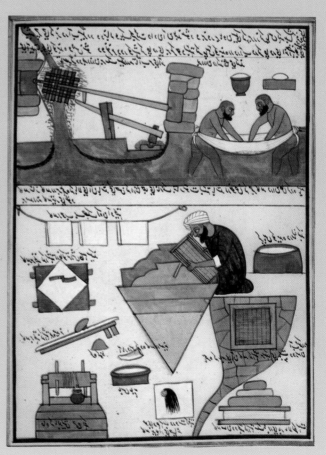

Discoveries and Inventions

Beginning in the 1400s, there were many new inventions in papermaking. Johannes Gutenberg (ca. 1400–68) printed a version of the Bible in Mainz, Germany, in 1455. Gutenberg printed 180 copies: 135 on paper and 45 on **vellum** (parchment made from calfskin). Later that century, papermaking spread to England.

The first paper mill in the United States was built in Philadelphia in 1690. Papermaking changed dramatically in the middle of the nineteenth century, when new steam-powered machines started turning out six times as much paper as hand-operated mills.

Johannes Gutenberg checks a page that has just come off his new printing press.

Learning from Wasps

The French scientist René Antoine de Réaumur (1683–1757) learned a lot by studying insects. He noticed that wasps used a type of paper to build their nests. Female wasps first chewed tiny pieces of wood from trees or timber. They wet the wood with **saliva**, making a pulp for their papery nest. In the eighteenth century, papermakers still used mainly linen and cotton rags for the fibers to make pulp. Despite Réaumur's discovery, human papermakers did not start using wood pulp on a large scale until the middle of the nineteenth century. This happened when new machines started making large quantities of paper very quickly, and new forms of pulp were needed.

French Machines

In 1798, French inventor Nicholas Louis Robert (1761–1828) invented a machine that could produce paper in a long sheet. Nine years later, two English brothers,— Henry (1766–1854) and Sealy Fourdrinier (1774–1847)—built an improved version. The early machines left the paper wet at the

Paper is still made in the traditional way at a working water-powered mill in central France.

end of the process, so it had to be hung up to dry. Machine-makers soon added steam-driven drying rollers, so the paper was ready to use at the end of the process. The French inventor Marc Isambard Brunel (1769–1849) called the Fourdriniers' machine "one of the most splendid inventions of the age."

More and More Paper

The first Fourdrinier machine in the United States started working in 1827. The new technology produced a huge amount more paper: in 1810, 3,300 tons (3,000 t) of paper were made in the U.S. Thirty years later, papermakers were making about ten times as much. By 1900, this had increased to 2.2 million tons (2 million t).

SPEEDING UP

By the 1860s, improved Fourdrinier machines were turning out 98 feet (30 m) of paper a minute. By 1900, the best machines were twice as fast. Later in the twentieth century, machines could produce more than 4,900 feet (1,500 m) of paper every minute.

Raw Materials

The main raw material for today's paper is wood. Papermakers also use cellulose fibers from other woody plants, such as straw, sugar cane, esparto grass, bamboo, flax, hemp, and jute. Today, high-quality writing and art papers are still made from cotton and linen fibers.

Years ago, wood arrived at the pulp or paper mill from a nearby forest as large logs. Tree trunks were taken to the mill by rail or road. Sometimes they were hauled to the nearest river and floated to the mill.

There the first job was to remove the bark, which contains fewer fibers than wood. Today, the bark is usually used as **biofuel** and is burned to generate steam and drive machinery. Modern mills use wood chips

Logs float downriver to a pulp mill in Ontario. The workers in the boat sort the logs as they move along.

In this traditional French mill, huge wooden stampers (or hammers) pound wet rags for 36 hours to turn them into pulp for papermaking.

rather than logs. Wood-chipping machines with large, strong blades can reduce logs to small pieces just an inch (2.5 cm) across.

Paper from Rags

For centuries, the main raw materials used in papermaking were cotton and linen rags. They were often bought from a local rag merchant (or rag-and-bone man) and taken to a paper mill's rag house. There, workers took off buttons and other fasteners before sending the rags to the **beater house**, where they were beaten by water-powered **stampers**.

Papermakers still use clean rags to make papers which are especially strong and durable. These include bank notes, certificates, art paper, and high-quality stationery. Today most of the rags we put in recycling boxes are used in a different way. High-quality textiles are sent to developing countries to be used for clothes. Low-quality rags are shredded and used as mattress fillers or industrial fabrics.

RENEWABLE RESOURCE

Trees are a renewable resource as long as forests are well managed. This means that foresters need to plant new trees to replace the ones they cut down and avoid cutting down too many trees at a time. An international organization called the Forest Stewardship Council (FSC) adds its logo to paper made from trees that are harvested in the least damaging way. The FSC controls more than 269 million acres (109 million **hectares)** of forest around the world.

RECYCLE RECYCLE RECYCLE RECYCLE

Making Pulp

Raw materials are turned into pulp for papermaking at a pulp mill. This may be part of a paper mill or a separate building on the same site. At the pulp mill, the wood is turned to pulp in one of three different ways.

This large pulp mill in Florida pumps out steam and smoke as it turns wood to pulp.

The three ways of making pulp are mechanical, chemical, and semichemical. All separate cellulose fibers from **lignin**, the natural substance that keeps the fibers together. Then the cellulose fibers are mixed with water to form a pulp.

Ground by Machines

The first pulp mills ground wood against slabs of sandstone, which were turned by

HOW MANY TREES?

You need about 13 trees—each about 40 feet (12 m) tall—to produce one ton of pulp by the mechanical process. You need about twice as many trees to make the same amount of pulp by the chemical (kraft) process. The mechanical process uses a lot of electricity—about 10,000 **megajoules** to make one ton of pulp.

This wood pulp has been bleached to make whiter paper.

water wheels. Today, the stones have been replaced by rotating steel discs, which grind wood chips against a fixed plate. The chips may be heated first to make them easier to grind. Ground wood pulp produces paper that tends to go yellow as it gets older. This is mainly used for newsprint, the low-quality paper on which newspapers are printed.

Using Chemicals

Chemicals can dissolve the lignin that holds wood fibers together. To do this, the chipped wood is heated in water with various chemicals. One method is called the **sulfate** (or kraft) process. This produces the most pulp around the world. The chemicals **sodium hydroxide** (lye) and **sodium sulfide** cook the chips in a steam-heated tank called a **digester**. The chemical processes produce all sorts of different papers.

A semichemical process uses both methods. First the papermaker uses chemicals to soften the wood chips, which a machine then grinds up. **Corrugated** cardboard and cheap printing paper is made in this way.

Bleaching

Papermakers **bleach** some pulps to produce whiter, brighter paper. The chemicals used can damage the environment, and many pulp mills have changed the way they bleach so they do not pollute lakes or rivers. Some older pulp mills have closed to prevent pollution, such as the mill beside Lake Baikal, in Russia, the world's deepest lake.

PULP FICTION

Books have been recycled for centuries. In 1883, an article in the *Fortnightly Review* magazine said, "Many unsaleable books are wasted, that is, are sent to the mill, ground up, pulped down, and made again into paper." By "wasted," the writer meant recycled. Cheap novels and magazines that were printed on low-quality paper were known as pulp magazines and pulp novels.

At the Paper Mill

The pulp that arrives at the paper mill is called stock. To prepare it for papermaking, it is beaten in a large mixing machine, which helps the fibers stick together. Sometimes starch or clay is added, depending on the type of paper being made. Then the pulp passes between turning blades in a machine called a refiner. This trims the fibers and makes them more flexible.

Once the pulp has been refined, it may be mixed with other things to make special papers, or dye is added to make colored paper. Then the stock is ready for the papermaking machine.

The Wet Stage

The papermaking machine mixes pulp and water and spreads it across a moving wire screen. The water drains through the vibrating wires, leaving a mat of fibers on the screen. Heavy rollers then squeeze more water from the wet mat and press it into

A fast, efficient machine produces large rolls of paper at a modern paper mill in Sweden.

Who Makes the Most?

The United States makes the most paper and wood pulp. China imports more wood pulp than it produces, but it also uses a lot of recycled paper. Canada exports nearly one-half the wood pulp it produces.

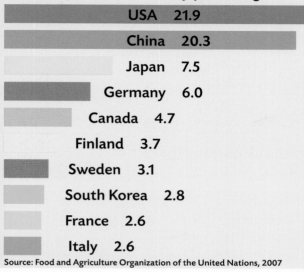

World Paper Production, by percentage

Country	Percentage
USA	21.9
China	20.3
Japan	7.5
Germany	6.0
Canada	4.7
Finland	3.7
Sweden	3.1
South Korea	2.8
France	2.6
Italy	2.6

Source: Food and Agriculture Organization of the United Nations, 2007

World Wood Pulp Production, by percentage

Country	Percentage
USA	29.5
China	3.6
Japan	6.1
Germany	1.7
Canada	12.9
Finland	7.3
Sweden	7.1
South Korea	0.2
France	1.3
Italy	0.3

Source: Food and Agriculture Organization of the United Nations, 2007

a smooth sheet. It goes through more rollers before moving to the drying section.

Drying and Smoothing

The wet sheet goes through a series of steam-heated cylinders. Then more substances may be added. Coating the surface of the paper by adding **resins**, starches, or chalks can make it more waterproof, stronger, shinier, and better for printing. Finally, the sheet is smoothed by passing through a stack of rollers called calenders. The machine then winds the finished dry sheet onto large reels, ready to be sent to printers and other manufacturers.

Swedish Papermaking

Papermaking has been important in Sweden for hundreds of years. The Holmen Paper company opened its first mill making handmade paper in 1633 in the town of Norrköping. Its first water-driven paper machine started in 1837. Today, the company has three machines in nearby Braviken, using spruce wood and recycled pulp. They produce 854,300 tons (775,000 t) of 28-foot (8.5-m) wide reels of newsprint a year.

LONG AND FAST

Paper machines can be 443 feet (135 m) long from beginning to end reel. They can produce up to 5,905 feet (1,800 m) of paper per minute, which means that the whole papermaking cycle can take less than 5 seconds.

Many Types of Paper

Papermakers have different names for the types of paper they produce. There are also names and codes for different sizes and weights of paper. Large books such as dictionaries and Bibles are printed on a thin book paper. Paper for printing needs a special finish, especially if color illustrations are printed on it.

Bond and Bank

Bond paper is high-quality business paper. It is strong and hard-wearing and used for printed letterheads (letter-size paper with a printed name on top) and letters. It may be different colors, such as gray or beige. White bond is used in computer printers. Bank paper is similar, but much thinner.

Coated Papers

Coating gives paper a smooth finish for printing—gloss, matte, satin, or silk. The finish on machine-coated papers is put on by the paper machine (see page 15). Off-machine coating is put on by separate machines immediately after the paper is made. Glossy paper goes through an extra series of rollers called a supercalender. This is good for printing books and magazines in color.

A worker checks the finished paper's quality in an American mill.

Watermarks

A watermark is a faint pattern you see when you hold paper up to the light. High-quality writing papers have a watermark which might show the brand or name of the maker.

Bank notes and certificates sometimes use a face as a watermark, which shows that the note is genuine. The mark is made by a pattern of wires on a roller in the papermaking machine.

WHAT DOES PAPER WEIGH?

In the United States, paper weight appears as pounds (lb.) per ream (500 sheets). A sheet of letter-size 20 lb. copy paper weighs .04 pound. Paper weight appears as grams per square meter (gsm) outside the United States. A sheet of 80 gsm copy paper (A4 size) weighs 5 g.

THE PAPER IN THIS BOOK

The paper this book is printed on was made in the United States. The name of the paper is Fortune Matte text and it weighs 80 lb.

International Paper Sizes

The international paper size standard (ISO 216) has been adopted by all countries except the United States. and Canada. The most common paper size outside the United States is A4 which measures 8.27 x 11.69 inches (210 x 297 mm). Most paper is sold in sizes ranging from the largest (A0) to the smallest (A7). All sizes are the same shape with each succeeding size exactly half the size of the previous one. For example, when you fold an A4 sheet in half, it makes two A5 sheets.

Paper for Packaging

Cardboard is simply thick paper, and it is also made on paper machines. You see cardboard everywhere, in packaging, as cartons and other containers, and as backing for writing pads and envelopes.

Paperboard

Cardboard that is more than 0.010 inches (0.25 mm) thick is called paperboard. One type called boxboard is used to make boxes and cartons for food and household products. These packages range from breakfast cereals and toothpaste to cartons for milk or orange juice. The cardboard can easily be printed, so companies can advertise on their containers. Many supermarkets ask their food suppliers to make their packaging attractive, so more shoppers will buy their products.

Corrugated Cardboard

Have you noticed that some large boxes are made of more than one layer of cardboard?

Opposite: Workers control and check production in a cardboard-box factory.

Corrugated cardboard protects products when they are transported. It is strong enough to absorb impacts and stop the contents from being damaged.

A corrugated container starts off as rolls of paperboard. Two boards are joined in the middle by a corrugated (wavy) board called a flute. This is made by a machine which pushes the flat board into ridges. The flute is glued inside the two boards, called liners, leaving air in the space between them. This acts as a **shock absorber**. The corrugated cardboard is then cut into the right shape, before being folded and glued into a box.

You can see the wavy flutes inside these pieces of corrugated cardboard, which are used to make boxes.

PAPER PRODUCTS

Lots of household products are made of paper. Here are just a few. You can probably think of many more.

coffee filters	disposable diapers
grocery bags	egg cartons
lampshades	paper plates and cups
paper towels	place mats
shoeboxes	tea bags
toilet paper	wallpaper
coasters	napkins

RECYCLING PACKAGING

Environmentalists want us to use less packaging. Often the packaging is there just to advertise a product, and packaging creates a huge amount of waste paper. In some countries, such as Germany, supermarket customers are encouraged to unwrap goods at the checkout after they have paid for them. They can then leave the unwanted packaging at the store, where it is collected for reuse or recycling.

Books and Bindings

Paper is ideal for writing, drawing, and printing on. Printing can quickly produce thousands of copies of writing or drawings—every one the same. In past centuries, printing inks were pressed onto paper. Today, most books are printed by a process called **lithography**.

This copy of the Diamond Sutra *was found in a Chinese cave in the early 1900s, more than 1,100 years after it was printed.*

Oil and Water

In 1796 an Austrian playwright named Alois Senefelder (1771–1834) polished a flat piece of limestone and wrote and drew on it with a greasy crayon. Then he wet the stone with water before putting ink on it. The ink stuck only to the drawing and writing. When he pressed paper against the stone, his design was transferred to the paper. Senefelder had discovered the idea of lithography (which means "stone writing").

Paper Sheets

Today, paper manufacturers cut rolls of paper into large sheets for printing. Each

FIRST PRINTED BOOK

The oldest printed book still in existence is probably the *Diamond Sutra*. This sacred Buddhist text was printed in China in 868 on paper made from mulberry bark, using carved wooden blocks. The copy in the British Library in London has seven strips of paper pasted together to form a scroll more than 16 feet (5 m) long. By the middle of the eleventh century, the Chinese were printing on paper with movable clay type. This meant that the letters that made up words could be moved around and reused.

An Indian printer checks the quality of political posters.

sheet is usually printed with 32 pages of the book (16 pages on either side). The printer puts a large stack of paper at one end of the printing press and then the sheets travel through the machine as they are printed. Different colors are printed one at a time, until the sheet is complete.

Folding and Binding

To finish a book, the printed sheets are fed into a folding machine. The pages are laid out in a particular order on the large sheet so that they are in the right order once the sheet is folded. Afterward the paper is trimmed to make the pages the right size and to separate the pages. Finally a machine binds the pages inside the cover.

PAPER, PAPER EVERYWHERE

Just over a million new books are printed and published around the world every year. The United Kingdom publishes more books than any other country in the world (21 percent of the total), followed by the United States (17 percent) and China (10 percent).

Creating with Paper

Many artists and designers create on paper: writing, drawing, and painting in sketch pads or on large pieces of art paper. Other artists use paper as part of their artwork, folding and building with it, or make paper by hand.

Handmade Paper

Some companies specialize in selling handmade paper. Some artists and designers make their own, working in the same way as the ancient Chinese, using a mold and a **deckle**. A mold is a frame covered with a screen. A deckle is a flat metal frame that covers the mold and contains wet pulp. It leaves an irregular or feathery edge on the paper, called a deckle edge. Some manufacturers copy this effect to make their machine-made paper look handmade.

Japanese Folding Paper

Origami is the traditional Japanese art of folding paper into shapes. The word origami means "folded paper" in Japanese. The traditional designs are often symbols of good luck such as cranes, lobsters, or tortoises. Today, people also make paper toys or houses from folded paper. Traditionally, origami is done with a square piece of paper, which is colored on one side, without cutting or pasting the paper. You can use ordinary copy paper, but in

This girl is learning origami by making paper cranes (a kind of bird).

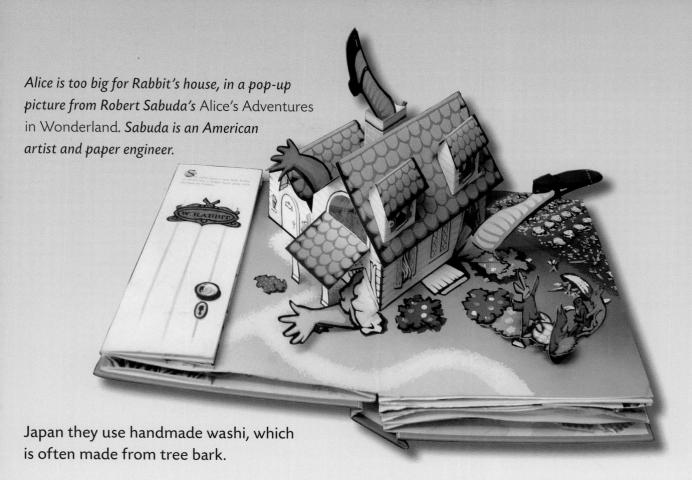

Alice is too big for Rabbit's house, in a pop-up picture from Robert Sabuda's Alice's Adventures in Wonderland. *Sabuda is an American artist and paper engineer.*

Japan they use handmade washi, which is often made from tree bark.

Paper Creations

Artists make collages by sticking pieces of paper and other **found objects** onto a backing paper. A German artist named Kurt Schwitters (1887–1948) created pictures from paper objects such as bus tickets, postage stamps, and pieces of newspaper. He became famous for his collage work, as well as for **graphic design** and **typography**. Many people have created similar works since, and some have even pretended that their works were done by Schwitters.

Paper Engineering

Paper engineers are designers who create pop-ups and other mechanical books. These first became popular in the 1800s, and many are printed today as novelty books for children. The books have tabs to pull, rings to turn, flaps to lift, and scenes that stand up from the page in three dimensions. Some use similar folding techniques to origami. The books are put together by hand, which makes them expensive to produce. The Movable Book Society, formed in 1993, shares knowledge among artists, collectors, designers, and book producers.

Using Waste

Pulp for handmade paper is usually made from cotton or silk waste. Sometimes waste from sugar cane or jute is used, too.

Reduce, Reuse, Recycle

There are many reasons for using less paper. First, making paper uses a lot of electricity. Most electricity is made by burning coal, oil, or natural gas, which puts waste gases into the Earth's atmosphere, causing pollution.

The pollution adds to the **greenhouse effect** and causes global warming. In the U.S., pulp and paper mills are some of the worst polluters of air, water, and land.

The Three Rs

We can all help to waste less paper by putting the three Rs into action. The letters stand for:

- reduce
- reuse
- recycle.

LOOK FOR RECYCLED PAPER

Office supply and discount stores sell paper that is made from recycled paper. Look for this and buy it when you can. Recycled paper is not usually bleached, so the paper might not be as white or bright as completely new paper, but fewer chemicals are used to make it, which is better for the environment.

Reducing means cutting down on waste by using less in the first place. We could reduce waste by using less paper packaging (see pages 18–19), and we could also reuse more paper. We could draw, write, or print on both sides of the paper we use. We could also fill the whole sheet before starting on

It's easy to collect used and waste paper. Then we can put it in a recycling bin.

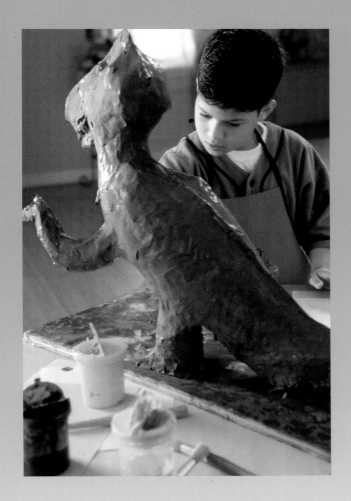

This boy is painting a model dinosaur made from papier mâché.

NEWSPAPERS FOR MODEL MAKING

Have you ever made a model with papier mâché? If so, you recycled paper to make something new. You can make papier mâché (which is French for "chewed paper") from torn strips of old newspapers. First soak the paper pieces in warm water to make pulp. Then mix it with wallpaper paste, glue, or flour and water to make a sticky mixture which can be shaped. As the papier mâché dries, it hardens. Once it is dry, you can paint it.

RECYCLE RECYCLE RECYCLE

another one. Finally, instead of throwing paper away in the trash can, we can put it in a recycling bin. Then, instead of being dumped in a landfill, the old paper will be reused to make new paper.

Instead of Trees

Another idea is to use more agricultural waste for making paper rather than cutting down so many trees. This waste can be used to make something called agri-pulp. A company in Costa Rica specializes in making paper from the parts of banana, coffee, and tobacco plants that are thrown away by other firms.

RECYCLE RECYCLE RECYCLE

WOMBAT WASTE

On the Australian island of Tasmania, a company makes paper from the droppings of one of Australia's favorite animals—the wombat. The wombat is a marsupial (which means that it has a pouch) and lives mainly in coastal forests where it feeds on plants, bark, and roots. Wombat dung contains a lot of fiber, which can be used to make pulp. The paper is popular with tourists.

Recycling Paper

Nearly one-half of all the paper we use has been recycled. Three kinds of scrap paper can be recycled. One is called "mill broke," which includes waste trimmings from paper mills. Another is called "preconsumer waste," which includes offcuts from printers, envelope trimmings, and rejected papers and printings. The third type is called "postconsumer waste," which is waste paper from offices and homes, old newspapers, and packaging.

The third type of scrap paper makes up the largest proportion of recycled paper, and it is collected from homes by garbage trucks or at neighborhood recycling centers.

Preparing and Cleaning

Waste paper often has different types of paper made from various fibers, including office waste paper, old newspapers, and cardboard. These are sorted before they are turned back into pulp. Recycled paper pulp can be used to make paper of the same or lower quality. Papermakers can't make higher quality paper unless they mix it with new pulp.

String, strapping, paper clips, staples, and other objects are removed from sorted

Machines have pressed waste paper into large bales at this recycling plant in France.

Waste paper is separated and sorted, ready to be turned back into pulp.

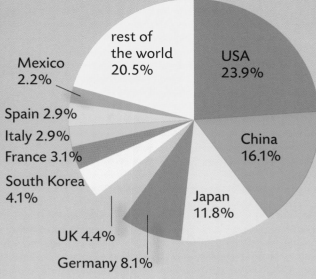

rest of the world 20.5%

Mexico 2.2%

Spain 2.9%

Italy 2.9%

France 3.1%

South Korea 4.1%

UK 4.4%

Germany 8.1%

Japan 11.8%

China 16.1%

USA 23.9%

Who Recycles the Most?

About 43 percent of all paper used around the world is recycled. The pie chart above shows the world's top producers of recycled paper. Together, the United States, China, and Japan make up more than one-half of the world's recycled paper total.

paper when bales arrive at a mill. A large magnet removes metal, and as the paper is pulped, a set of turning wires called a "ragger" catches pieces of string. Some pulp mills also use a hooked tool called a "junker" to fish out other unwanted items. Glue-based backing and binding materials are the most difficult to remove—these are called "stickies."

Washing Off the Ink

If ink spreads through recycled pulp, it can give it a gray tinge. Pulpers wash off ink by putting the paper in water with chemicals that separate the ink from the paper. They rinse the fibers several times, draining off the water between rinses. Another method is to add chemicals to the pulp and blow air through it to make foam and form a sticky froth on top. The air bubbles take the ink to the surface where the froth is removed.

A Paperless Future?

For years people thought that we would use less paper as we use computers more, but this has not happened. Today we use more paper than ever before. Will this change? Banks, phone, and fuel companies now send customers statements and bills directly to their computers, so they use less paper, and this may happen more in future.

Using Paper

In the world's rich, developed countries, most people use about 335 pounds (152 kg) of paper per year. This is 12 times more than people in developing countries, where people usually do not have enough paper. The countries that use most paper per person every year are Finland, the U.S., Canada, Belgium, and Japan.

Endless Recycling?

Today paper cannot generally be recycled more than six times, because the fibers grow shorter and weaker every time they are pulped. New pulp has to be added to keep up the strength and quality of the fibers. Perhaps future scientists will find a way to overcome this so that paper can be recycled endlessly.

People still use a lot of paper to print from their computers. Will this change in the future?

These fast-growing kenaf plants can be used to make paper.

Paper from Plants

The kenaf plant is similar to hemp and jute. It can grow to 16 feet (5 m) tall in just a few months. Traditionally people have made rope, twine, and coarse cloth from kenaf fiber, but recently it has been used to make paper. Experts believe that we could grow kenaf specially to make paper, as it is easier to grow and grows more quickly than trees. About 2.5 acres (1 ha) of kenaf can produce about 22 tons (20 t) of fiber for making paper in one season. The same area of pine forest produces about 6.6 tons (6 t) of fiber. Kenaf pulp is also whiter than wood pulp.

Will There Be Enough Wood?

We will probably need more and more wood for pulp in the next 50 years, but experts think that we do produce enough wood fiber for now. They calculate that the pulpwood we need could come from a plantation about 154,000 square miles (400,000 sq km) in size. This is an area slightly smaller than California.

MORE HELP FOR THE ENVIRONMENT

Today's environmental activists have some key goals for papermakers. They want

- more recycled pulp used to make paper
- people to use less paper and recycle more of what they use
- specially appointed organizations to look after forests
- stricter rules about how we use land, so forests are not turned into paper plantations
- no more chemicals used to bleach paper

RECYCLE RECYCLE RECYCLE RECYCLE

Glossary

beater house   A place in old paper mills where rags were beaten to make pulp.

biofuel   A fuel produced from biomass (plant or animal matter).

bleach   A substance used to whiten paper.

Buddhist   Related to Buddhism, a religion and philosophy founded in ancient India.

carbohydrate   A substance made up of carbon, hydrogen, and oxygen. Sugar, starch, and cellulose are carbohydrates.

carbon   A nonmetallic chemical element in coal and many other substances.

cellulose   A substance that makes up the cell walls of plants.

coniferous trees   Cone-bearing, needle-leaved trees, such as fir, pine, and spruce. Most conifers are evergreen and do not drop their leaves in autumn.

corrugated   Folded in ridges and grooves.

crusade   One of a series of holy wars in the Middle Ages. European Christian knights wanted to capture land in the Middle East from Muslim forces.

deckle   A flat metal frame that holds wet pulp during papermaking.

digester   A large tank in which substances are broken down by chemicals.

environmentalist   A person who looks after the natural environment.

esparto grass   A tough kind of grass with narrow leaves.

fibers   Tiny, thread-like plant cells.

flexible   Able to bend easily.

found objects   Things that artists find and use in their work, such as pieces of paper, metal, or cloth.

graphic design   The art of combining printed words and pictures, especially in books and magazines.

greenhouse effect   Warming of the Earth's surface caused especially by pollution from burning fossil fuels (coal, gas, and oil).

hardwood   The kind of wood that comes from broad-leaved trees, such as birch or oak.

hectare (ha)   A unit of area the same as 2.5 acres (10,000 sq m).

hemp   A woody plant that can be used for making paper and rope.

hydrogen   A light, colorless gas that combines with oxygen to make water.

jute   A tropical plant with tough fibers.

kilowatt hours (kWh)   An amount of electrical energy (the same as 1,000 watts) used in one hour.

lignin   A substance that holds plant fibers together and makes plants rigid and woody.

lithography   A printing process using a flat surface (or plate) on which words and pictures take up greasy ink that can then be pressed onto paper.

megajoule   A unit of energy (one million joules).

mold   A hollow container that shapes a wet or molten substance when it hardens.

oxygen   A colorless gas that humans and animals need to breathe to live.

pollution Damage to the environment caused by harmful substances.

pulp A wet, slushy mass of fibers that is used to make paper.

resin A sticky substance produced by some plants.

saliva Watery liquid produced in the mouth; spit.

shock absorber Something that takes in (or absorbs) jolts and bumps, to protect something else from damage.

sodium hydroxide A burning substance that is used in making paper, soap, and other materials; also called lye or caustic soda.

sodium sulfide A substance used to break down wood fibers and make pulp.

softwood The kind of wood that comes from coniferous trees, such as fir or pine.

stamper A heavy wooden hammer used in paper mills to beat rags and make pulp.

starch A white substance from plants that can be used to stiffen things.

sulfate A chemical substance that contains the elements sulfur and oxygen.

typography The art and process of arranging letters and words to be printed.

vellum Parchment (a flat material for writing on) made from calfskin.

Web Sites

Facts and statistics on the paper industry and products by the American Forest and Paper Association.
http://www.afandpa.org/PulpAndPaper.aspx

UCSD site on how to make paper.
http://gort.ucsd.edu/preseduc/papermak.htm

History, instructions on making paper, folding origami and shapes at The Paper Project at Arizona State.
http://paperproject.org

Articles on papermaking and the environment from the Ecology Global Network.
http://www.ecology.com/features/paperchase/index.html

History of British mills and diagram of the Fourdrinier machine.
http://www.hertfordshire-genealogy.co.uk/data/topics/t093-paper-makers-apsley.htm

Index